AZIMUTH

poems

Rachel Tzvia Back

Sheep Meadow

AZIMUTH

AZIMUTH

Rachel Tzvia Back

THE SHEEP MEADOW PRESS
RIVERDALE-ON-HUDSON, NEW YORK

Inquiries and permission requests should be addressed to:
The Sheep Meadow Press
PO Box 1345
Riverdale-on-Hudson, NY 10471

The opening denotations of "azimuth" are from Lane's *Arabic-
English Lexicon*, 1872, and from the *Oxford English Dictionary*.
"Gravity & Grace" takes its title and opening lines from Simone
Weil's essay of the same name. The epigraph for "Litany" ("...so
many voices, there") is from Gustaf Sobin's "Lineage" in *Voyaging
Portraits* (New Directions 1984). In "Azimuth (IV)" the poems
quoted are as follows: "We travel like other people...," "Speak
speak..." and "country of words..." from Mahmoud Darwish's poem
"We Travel Like Other People" in *Modern Poetry of the Arab World*,
translated by Abdullah al-Udhari (Penguin 1986); "What happened
really happened" and "distant bell..." from T. Carmi's "Author's
Apology" in *At the Stone of Losses*, translated by Grace Schulman
(JPS 1983). "I believe with perfect faith..." is the opening formula
of a Hebrew prayer affirming one's belief in the Messiah's arrival.
"The heart is the toughest part..." is from Carolyn Forche's
"Because One Is Always Forgotten" in *The Country Between Us*
(Harper & Row 1981).

The Library of Congress Cataloging-in-Publication Data

Back, Rachel Tzvia, 1960-
   Azimuth / Rachel Tzvia Back.
p. cm.
    ISBN 1-878818-95-3 (alk. paper)
    I. Title.

PS3552.A2579 A98 2001
811'.6--dc21   00-069853

ACKNOWLEDGMENTS:

Earlier versions of many of these pieces first appeared in *The American Poetry Review*, *Apex of the M*, *ARC*, *Bridges*, *Dark Ages Clasp the Daisy Root*, *Modern Poetry in Translation*, *Sulfur*, *The Tel-Aviv Review*, *Tikkun* and in the anthology *Dreaming the Actual: Contemporary Fiction and Poetry by Israeli Women Writers* (SUNY Press, 2000).

I wish to thank to Shirley Kaufman, Peter Cole and Nita Schechet for their support, suggestions and great generosity of spirit.

azimuth: from Arabic *as-sumut* the azimuth, plural of *as-samt* the way—commonly relating to the course one pursues in journeying. An Arab of the desert, of the tribe of Keys says: *Thou shalt traverse (addressing a woman) a land without a description, journeying without any sign of the way and without any track, such being the meaning of as-samt.*

an arc of the heavens extending from the zenith to the horizon which it cuts at right angles; a point of the compass as measured clockwise from the north point 0° through 360°.

Contents:

5

I

Gravity & Grace

I
A beloved disappoints me.
I speak to him.
Impossible he should not

reply by saying what I
have said to myself
in his name.

The debt of the one
desired (far corner of
a crib, a room, an unforgotten

not-father) is as wide as
the visible horizon
as great as

desire itself.
To accept that
he is other than

first comforter,
certain shelter,
exclusively

mine
is to imitate
the renunciation,

admit all covenants
are broken (heifer,
she-goat and ram

in bloody pieces
laid out
gently

in the dirt)
at the moment they
are made.

The only truth of
the beginning.

2

Across from each other
in a closed room: were either
to stretch out, their feet

would touch. They don't.
She is crying.
He is saying, as though

from a great distance
"Can you hear me?"
as though

she cannot, deafened
as she is by the din
of what is breaking.

He is saying "I have
lost you"
as though she has

strayed, as though
she could be found.
In the thicket.

Horns entangled, not
a sound. Wide-eye stare,
neck bent low, knows

not to look up, bright
zodiacal light
betrayed.

Only the ash-colored ram
remains, limbs
aching in self-

enforced stillness
to not be
the burnt-offering

(rampant faith, thickest
weeds) not
bleed in the stead of.

Atop an appointed mountain,
so close were either
to stretch out a hand, they would

touch. They don't. Father, his
son, and me.

3
My father, the blue-eyed Canaanite,
rests his heavy hands
on my head, weight

of all he wants
bearing down
on me

beyond blessing.
His words—
raspy, ragged—

and world
dissolve into component
parts, will not

cohere. His handprint
permanent, though I would
hide it.

My father, Semitic dweller
from the farthest Southern Cape,
velvet voice believer,

watches from the wings
presses fingertips
together as in

partial prayer, then
open his hands
wide (will

not touch)
and says
"there are moments

of grace, good hope,
passage back—that
should be enough"

and wanders off. My
father, imagined father,
darkest Assyrian

from the far north
in the ruins of the town
I loved best

digs up graves by day,
waits for flares
by night, to light

warfare or return.
He says "you and I
have to be willing

to have our hearts
broken."

4
The past breaking out
in my heart: the text
yields, work and wonder

with the interpreter, pain
mine. I sleep entire
days away, I wait

for nothing. The invisible
realms were not formed in love
but in fear. Fear and desire

in a closed room: he
keeps her close, she
(still in the midst

smallest in the sea)
cannot stay
cannot leave.

Dark bodies beneath
begin to pull, all movement
of the heart (hundred

meters from shore
land becoming nothing,
shore moving

away) controlled by dark
gravity: central force, first
demands

(underwater rock
false foothold
in a fluid world—

unbeliever, her ankle
ribboned with red
only sign of the struggle)

unfathomed, unmet, arms
still outstretched

5
A sheep slaughtered
at the threshhold
on imagined

homecoming:
I step over
the pool of black blood

into a darkened room where
my not-father
awaits, away

from the women's
rising cries
outside. The warm

soft carcass
is left at the doorstep.
I know

I am also other
than what I imagine
myself to be—

Hard
unforgiving (she-
goat or ash

ram amid thorns, rough
brush) in an empty
room (empty

refrain, prayer,
promise,
hill, or

hold)   absence
the core

6
Across from each
other in a closed
room.

She sits rigid, reclaimed.
She is iron, or ice.
She is saying "this

is the downward
motion inherent
in certain bodies.

Protest proves useless—
therefore, you must
love me."

He
is saying "grace
will fill empty

spaces, create
possibility of
ascendance, or

acceptance" (smoke
smelling of sweet
sweet wood, driest

words, deception and sweat,
spirals upward).
A beloved

listens closely
(weak
bleating of first dumb

beasts).   I
am silent, my
body in deepest

sleep
my body still
as self

accelerates
toward what

never
stops hurting

—————

2

There Were Boats (Water)

There were boats on black waves
boats of black waves just beyond
the black border, waiting to pull
to shore, pull us to sea.

You held a white stone, chose
a black one for me. Too smooth,
it slipped from my palm into night's.

Men of fisherboats, patrolboats. No one spoke
the same language, only black salt
encrusted words. On shore, we heard

nothing, smelled wet ropes and sweat.
Past moon down, we thought we saw nets
glistening and sudden sparks on the water

where prow lamps may sway.
But by the lowest stars we caught
glints of guns too. Black metal shining.

You hummed, sand slipping under sea.
You did not say *love*:
the stone, the one I lost, was all.

You believed there were boats

just beyond the water border.
I believed they were black
and there were waves, waiting

Elementary Landscapes (Fire)

There was the smell of fire on her clothes,
as though she were always just returning.
From the street, from the rails,
from feeding some flame for hours.

There was the smell of fire, and that flat
certainty to her face. As though she were
still staring, frozen, into some turning
torch or siren. Some tangled light.
On the street, on the rails, the black

of her eyes opened, and her skin tight.
I can tell you I saw smoke in her hair,
underneath the matted black. As though
she were just returning. Actual wool
strands of thick grey and white stirring.

I knew of the fields she might have come from.
The fireweed high there in the burnt-over
areas, tight tufts of its purple flowers
flashing. From feeding some flame for hours.
And on her skin layers of dust:

behind her ears, beneath her breasts.
Even on her breath. Or maybe it was ash.
Her nails black, jagged. They were broken.

From the street, from the rails.
She slept with her eyes half open.

The bruise under her right collar bone
eventually turned yellow at the edges. Frozen.
And under the hair on her calves and thighs,
under the skin, there were slender black thorns
she didn't seem to feel. She never said

anything, and I never pulled them out, though
I burned the tip of a needle black in the stove's
blue flame. She seemed still to be staring
into some turning light. Even while she slept.
The smoke in her hair stirring. And that flat

certainty to the face. From the street, or
from the fields. As though just returning.
Maybe it was the dust, or some tangled light.
Still, I must tell you of the smell of fire.

Elementary Landscapes (Air)

He cannot remember the flight
still lives suspended across

skies; absented as he fell,
nor the earth to return to.

The birds were wingless,
their bodies dark bullets

in flight patterns pulling
toward borders crossed

in disguise. He cannot remember
why, nor tell of the still lives

suspended in the others' eyes, nor
how his body at war with space

fell. But he heard his legs break
at impact and someone call, crossing

borders in the dark, in disguise.
His broken pattern pulling the eye

elsewhere. Not there, nor was I
earth to return to. Still

the skies measured my mind
over borders, dark birds without

wings, and his splintered breathing
pulling us earthward.

Litany (I)

" . . . so many voices, there,"

but not one loud enough to hear (close the door
quietly, sound travels) as more than motion:

a train passing (we'll wait here until there is
better reason to leave) or the bells' ringing

carried by rain across a city (the year's first
flooding in the flat lands) unhinged and always

preparing itself (they dressed in white for both
prayer and death) for the next siege (caves,

under the poppy fields)

while we, you and I, have been preparing ourselves
for speech (always a light on at the gate) since

first we fell silent. Not knowing what will heal
(trapped in byways, between endings) or what will

name (electrical current cut) us in the blackouts,
we look for traces in the dark of what has been

said (wear no leather when you are in mourning)

though only the chiming of the bells from the empty

church can cross the city.

He could not hear us, as children, when we came
 (carry the candlesticks, wrap them in white linen)

to say goodbye before leaving the country, and he
(to heal: first name the disease) was yellow from

lung cancer and would be dead long before, and if,
we returned (echoing through the damp passageways

between caves: caverns, storage wells, dark
sanctuaries. small chambers with sloping stairs),

not tied to this or any other continent.

An illusion of belonging (we come from a long
line of women who hated themselves) and no other

longing (unhinged) but for order in the voices
that storm (the last train left weeks ago)—

we've been away longer than those markers (don't
forget the hour of candlelighting) show, languages

forgotten (in secret closets, in musty cellars)
though a memory of the source, somewhere between

heart and throat, remains.

The coffin was put on the next plane (remember her
long years of depression, hands shaking) as he had

wanted to be buried in holy dirt (at home) and when
the van pulled into the courtyard (an equidistance

between two continents), the only sound was our
old aunt (to heal: first name the disease) wailing,

running alongside the van as it slowed (among
blackcoated strangers) and stopped, she was wailing

(stone and black strokes)

and screaming at her dead brother who had never
returned. She, with all the women (his body wrapped

in white, lighter than hollow bones) not allowed to
go to the cemetery, but the rabbi ripped her black

blouse across its worn collar (tear your clothes
in mourning, sit seven days) and she wouldn't stop

wailing. This isn't about travel: only in which
strange city (Thessaloniki, Palmyra) did we, you

and I, first fall silent?

Voices from the east, (the tracks are rusted and no
longer used) where meaning lies in the inflection

of the silence (seeds dried in the sun), in the
strange accents we speak (wait for the third star

before you light fire) and never fully recognize
(to heal: first name the disease) as our own

(sins committed with words) - only the motion of
sound (her dry tongue after the shock treatment)

am I sure of.

As to the crowded litanies (she sewed snaps on half
made skirts, dime a dozen) in the places of prayer

and in the markets, I can only record: crossroads,
train whistles, letters opened in public places,

the push (wear white, no leather) of so many voices
there, but not one clear enough to hear (across

the river in Petra), so much silence in that dark
space (beside the red rock) between desire and

dying and (what will name us)

Litany (II)

"so many voices, there,
vie for the
            voice . . . "

and leave you
silent.

Neither sand nor prayer.

I am sorry:

as daughter
understanding less

what desire *disappointed*
will not loosen

its hold, or let
sleep. 5 a.m.:

you are walking around the lake.

Come back later and tell us
of the heron   shrieking,
her wings   weighted with ice.

———————

What no one else saw.

How you stowed away
in the dark hull of a boat
smuggling arms into Palestine.

Now only language will not travel,
across similar borders,
in black, in kefeyiah,

so you try to translate the memory.

Young man in uniform,
on the shores of a new Babel
among survivors who knew
no speech

would do

and fell silent.

———————

Another walled city in ruins.

Not sand, not prayer.

At the British mental hospital
in Tiberias where stationed,

the mad from shellshock

screamed at night down
the green corridors, called
into the empty streets.

You walked by the water
after blackout
that jasmine

by the rare iron gate
locked wild
against another night.

———————

Always in between

countries, across oceans.
En route and arriving

at the airport
as the gate closes:

coming back to us

with ancient atlases and miniature
globes for the boys,
large dolls for the girls: we

wanted you not to leave
us behind,

were not trained for travel.

your three dark daughters
blue-eyed and green,
three solemn daughters crying.

———————

So I cannot ask

between sand and prayer

what have you wanted,
and from whom.

In some foreign city, your heart
straying and you

collapsed by the baggage check,
black briefcase in hand.

Across an ocean and over
a phone line
black water

storming over the deep laid wire.

Later you told us you said psalms
through the night
before surgery *heard*

your dead parents praying.

———————

I have seen you

empty your pockets
into the sea, believing

with crumbs and lint, your sins
would sink.

Now you ask:
in the Book of Life
or Book of Death?
so many voices,

here, come back,
your dead parents praying.

You listen, not of one
mind, to a new moon

three solemn daughters all in green
in three separate cities crying

and your new heart *storming*

over the deep laid wire.

Litany (III)

"so many voices, there,
vie for the
  voice, crowd sound with the white
pressure of
their

silence."

———————

I
The scar: a bare and rocky place
on a mountain side, or some other
steep slope.

Where the body was divided, opened
no longer at peace under the one
silent sky.

What would grow *something*
on a ridge.

2

He left Sarah alone with two children
and still refused to give her the "get"
how the body was deserted, was bare
and would not open

that would have freed her to remarry.
Sarah alone in her parents' house,
a silent place that would not open
again to another

doing the books for the rich cousins,
dying early.

Her daughter, my mother, once sent us
alone to meet him, small man
absence of love on a steep slope, in
a rocky place

with round glasses, in a high domed room.
Later, she kept one folded black notice
the land yellow and sitting low
against the sky

but would not sit the seven days
of mourning for his death.

3

Five children of this lineage. I am one
or another steep slope, a bare and
rocky place.

The scar: what protects, what remains
under the one, smoke colored sky.

———————————

Litany (IV)

As the tale is told
too much was known.

So, just before birth
the last angel pressed her finger
across our lips, and said: "Shh...

don't tell." See the mark? There,
that soft hollow over your mouth.

3

After Eden

We slept on the edge of town, in the last building
before the desert. Freight trains carried salt
all night through our sleep, rusted boxcars
from forty years before clanging north, then south
at the edge of town. We could have forgotten
that wandering, but there were still dreams
of thirst and yellow winds.

By dark morning, our car parked in the last serpentine
light of the last streetlamp, our eyes narrowing as we
neared, we saw late the side window shattered
around a hole at the center: Cain's splintered
web across our foreheads in the glass.
We could have forgotten that mark, still
stunned to be so far from Eden.

A Different Desert

In a desert
different from those I had imagined
hills glinted with shattered shells
from distant seas, and strange stiff
shrubs grew in dry riverbeds.
No sand dunes shifted with winds:
there was no wandering
in this desert, no
leaving. When at dusk
I thought I was nearing a border,
darkness swept jagged hills
higher into night, black
winds carried voices
away.

      I, of uneven breathing
deep within that desert,
pressed body to a cold ground and listened
to the cackle of dry bush
while a late yellow moon
and shivering stars thralled
east in an arc far above my head.
It was earth
with no memory of day.

Beyond the western hill
in that desert I have not imagined

lies a valley pockmarked
by shells, covered with bullet casings.
The silence there is shallow;
the wild ones, wary.

Unplaited

This stranger love took us
across unmarked borders
to lands that fold at dusk
and know no light till morning,
tin-pitched sheep bells
swaying to the slow gait
of first darkness and
fading.   Lands where winds

suddenly rise in mid-night
twirl their stiff unplaited
braids, as suddenly
die. Love traced there
between my breasts
strange letters
and other routes back.

Strange, love taken root
along dark footpaths stretching
white over night slopes into
unnamed valleys and we too
were nameless with so many

names not our own.   A love
of distance, of thorn bushes
torn from earth easily but

stubborn nonetheless, tangled
and belonging nowhere.

O but here, where we've tagged
each hilltop, have touched
no one unknown, you and I

seem to have no need
for the other,
and we've forgotten
the common language
neither spoke.

We never knew so much
could be lost
to a foreign land.

Notes: from the Wait

I

No nameable danger to the season.

The heat an absence of air absence

of desire. Behind doors we painted

white we pull shades low   move slow:

let others stake out their territory.

What we have lost will stay lost

last half moon buried under.

I know now we belong

to no part of this landscape.

2

At night the road to the capital

disappears.

Mountains bulldozed and abandoned

open to the sun and slow deaths

move together to console.

Displaced dirt red at first

unearthing returns dry and dark

ingathering of the exiled

All our markings sword to stone

are vanishing

3

We of a scorched generation

while night nets in its stars

And the half-drained swamp

returns to swamp.

Musk smell of hot trees in water

thickening like fire: land

of pale wood pyres.

Through smoke darkness I hear

drum murmurs over the valley:

the sacrifice done   not done

4

Dawn

White hillside boulders

gather forces to storm city walls:

stone on stone on marked stone.

Last deafening insurrection

as splintered city gates burn.

Far from home at home no one

speaks now of exiles

that will end

5

You are right to stay away.

Those prayers on the doorpost

will protect no one.

As to why we remain:

we're busy now

waiting

behind bolted doors

for the season that will not pass

to pass

Gaza, undated:

I

After the final heave, house collapsing
in and all the prayers that had held
the ceiling up for years rushing
through dust with a low moan
but leaving, you have seen her
sifting through the rubble,
sandaled foot striking an iron
bedframe, splintered picture
of a prophet's resting place.
With no tears you have seen her,
dry like stone, like tile,
and alone.

Then understand the law as I did not:
We tore her house down. *Her kitchen smelled of zatar
and of warm bread.* She may not rebuild
here or elsewhere.

2

Consider prayers' desertion and our faith
crushed where it was neatly tucked
between headscarves in the top drawer
even as our walls still stand:
*No believing now. Only children in the alleys,
their blood darkening the dirt.*

After the rains, this mound will settle, sink
in on itself and forget what it was.
She will not forget.

Seasons

Winter we raise
batons smash down
with full force
on their shoulders
arms and legs

break bones all
winter in alleys
and courtyards, pine
batons: best wood

of the Galilee
where all summer

the forests burn.

What Can Be Broken

"The heart is the toughest part of the body.
Tenderness is in the hands."

He is blindfolded when they break his fingers
easily, bones brittle in this cold,
and he cradles that hand in the other,
huddled by the wall. Winds slip past soldiers,
moan in the courtyards, and the women
watch from behind second-floor slats,
rocking themselves silent.

Do not ask now have these hands
stroked her back, will they stroke
her long back, crooked fingers
between the blades, and have these hands
held — do not ask what have they held
in the first crossed light of morning,
wooden picking pole or basket, do not
ask about the string of beads, the pen.

The skin swells and blackens, the bones will ache
every winter but will hold, this you must know,
the rock or gun more firmly. Tenderness
is in the hands. It can be broken.

From the Watertower

I
Amber
  before ash.

August.
All the forests burning.

From the watertower we watched
the oaks in agony
opening, dark wood splintered
bending slow o, burning, burning.

Redder hours, there were none.
The lynx, a late love,
watched over the fire.
I was not there, so
I would not know.
Only the yellow scorpion,
more poisonous than the black,
scuttled through the fire.

No deer, no sudden dashes out
as all were rooted and we

in the watertower
its hot metal shining.

2

Bronze
  before rust.

Bones black.
The forests slashed red.

Your face was tight from the heat,
flinched silently with the cackle
and crash: each dark collapse,
flames snapping at a severed sky.

Stars tried to pull back
but those touched at the tip
fell. The lynx, on a bare
capstone east of the fire,
listened to their light streak
the sky, a shriek I did not hear.
And the scorpion, of silent sting,
planned for a dark desert.

You placed your hands flat
on the watertower floor

to feel the vibration
of each tree's fall.

3
Coal
  after.

Cancer root uncovered.
Body and forest stripped bare.

By then you slept
in the curve of the tower
as though it were dusk
when the fire started to die.

Darker that dawn, only smoke rising.
The lynx, spotted fur thick,
padded alone among half-trees
I did not see.
And I could not tell
how he smelled the ash and crumbling.

What was a forest would not
calm itself, earth and air entangled

ensnared in death and dark
desire,

the scorpion unsinged.

Jerusalem Couplets

I

The horse flew because the stone
on which he stood was wet.

Under red rugs the stone
still is damp.

2

Soldiers on all the rooftops:
by the Sixth Station, where

she wiped his bloody brow, another
had his head blown off

last night, in the alley's
last light.

3

The seventh gate is blocked
with rubble and stones

hauled up from the valley
to stop the second, or third,

coming. The priestly stairs:
they lead nowhere.

4
The old road down to Jericho
was paved with gravestones.

Other small bodies are stolen
away from army mortuaries

wrapped in dark. Tell
how the children died.

No one will believe.

5
A faith that asks
no questions, is fed

by loss.
Keeps its eyes

and ears closed
through the telling.

4

Azimuth (I)

North
seven borders and
seven mists meet.

He faced east
bowed five times,
fingered the beads
and flew.

In the west
birds cluttered
the sky, skirted
three seas.

And she alone
to the South
opened her home.

Azimuth (II)

north

The mist, the mosque.

Barefoot
on the red weave
he faced
    east,
bowed five
times

and flew

blue beads falling
from the sky.

———————

south

She, skirt
in the sea
    sand
washed

tender at shore

Barefoot
on brown weeds

and hung the white
wings on the line

to sway

slowly in the bright
heat where borders
the beads like birds
blur.

Azimuth (III)

90°:
He never flew.

She was not barefoot.

Believe none of it.

The maps, folded and refolded,
frayed: entire ranges lost
at the creases.
The compass needle
in its own green light
pulled toward passing metals:
trains, tanks, satellites.

Their soles in thick boots
burned. Sweat welded skin
to shirt, to gun strap:
a damp, hot branding.

He hated most the birds
that slept in the low bushes
and flew

that slept in the low bushes

and flew at him with crowded fury
when he stumbled into their crossed
branches and quiet breathing,

sharp wings suddenly flung wide
in the dark, wider to his dark
wanting eye.

She hated the fields
when freshly turned
dirt clumps loose and thick

the fields when freshly turned

waiting in the dark
dirt clumps like claws
at her ankles, calves sore,
stumbling under the rough scorn
of unseen farmers, and her own
heavy breathing.

———————————

45°:
There were seven borders

and seven mists in the valley,

each thicker than the rest.

The three seas were low.

Collaborators flew
from rooftops.

Freedom fighters ground
stone into flour.

Everyone ate dust.

He was lost
and she

was lost.

Planning their route ahead
had done no good:

the land bore only scars

bore no resemblance
to lines on the map:

steeper, deeper

so much wider

with all the orchards
uprooted.

Azimuth (IV)

"We travel like other people, but we return to nowhere..."
Mahmoud Darwish

At the Stone of Losses,
another loss.

I, as half-stranger,
am the one who came
to call out the identifying marks
of what had been lost
but instead,
stood on the Stone
silent.

"What happened really happened."

I flew here.

I am the one
who pushed against gravel–

cut wind

sharp and savage
(jagged splinters from the Stone)

to enter the dark
helicopter hull, and forgot
your face immediately.
You who were a step behind.

"What happened really happened.

I believe with perfect faith"

there were stretchers
too heavy to carry,
there were bodies left behind.

Bodies

left behind
on a dark field:

this is a tale
that has never been told.

"I believe with perfect faith
that I will find the strength to believe
that what happened really happened."

———————————————

In the deafening ascent
both desert and sea were danger:

no lights, no stars to mark
where sky and land mingled

where sea and sky merged.

A sea that flies in the squall.

A desert as fertile:

floods with no warning.

All places of extremes.

I believe with imperfect faith

in faith imprecise
as these instruments,
fragments of the flight here.
I understood only the codes:

caves

constellations

our loss ringing in the dark.

"distant bell (he fell)
green pine (missing in action)
small cloud (captured)
bird's nest (wounded)"

There was blood on the boulders.

I am the one who
learned the maps last,
resigned first to fatigue,
would not believe

whose blood it was
on the whitest boulders.

At the Stone of Loss,
another loss.

A hovering above

what may be water, may be land
to return to

(slender, and still

so difficult to navigate)

"Speak speak so we may know the end of
this travel."

I, half stranger
at a stone
of loss

spoke for no one.

I am the one
who now speaks

(I have been to the barbed North)

in translations:

(the tel
is still
mined)

all I could carry.

Azimuth (V)

0° :
True North was a water god

who blurred borders:
seven brothers

and seven sisters
in the thickset mist

under a single oak.

The true north is never
as measured.

We have faced east
toward the last wall

toward the black stone.

We have circled 32 points.

We have returned
to nowhere

in this country of words.

Still, I must tell you

the compass rose
will yet invent

a new direction:

strange blossom.

Believe what you will.

5

Three Love Chants

I

Dark cedars of dark lebanon.
the ash, the oak.
the elm.   O,
the eucalyptus.

The apple (love) apple
(in the empty orchard)

(by the old graveyard)

2

Bone (like shell.
the colour of dry sand):
your breastbone (open
to touch. silver chain)
collar (twice broken.
where you are angles)
spine (a valley. damp.)

This bone (bold) remembering
every break.

3
Sound in the bone
at your breast
(like water)

far off (pushing
over pebbles, storming
down slopes, toward
the dry stone canyon
where I stand

darker than the cedars
and more fragrant.

August: Fragments

Benjamin
what would you now?

And if
I put my head here

your heart running?

———

Our silence under
the engine's rumble

for weeks
the metal burned.

At the end
you shaved your beard

your cheekbone bare.

———

My palms are dry.

You still want

sometimes
the simple prayer

though how many years
are you no longer
one of the quorum?

————

You bent over her
dark haired
at the gate

while I
on the walk up
the stone stairs
held another's hand

though it felt
just then like
you and I
only.

————

I have words you do not

but could also
not admit

through the open window

how the air
wavered in the heat.

————

Miles from

and the cherries
still wet in wicker baskets

children held
their rusted scales
by the road

pits hard and smooth
between our teeth and tongues.

————

What if then
Benjamin

now
my heart running?

Gravel Tones

We know only that he let go
of the rope and dove deeper.
His friends did not follow.
Panic emptied their tanks.
Now, those are *pearls*
that were their eyes.
His father waits daily
at the sea's edge
for the body that will not
wash up. *Drown, bright alto*
star: all cold and hunger
and claws. There is only
this dark tenorous sea:
gravel tones, black kelp,
constant longing.

We too watch for boats,
like a lighthouse, stroke
after stroke: terrorist dinghies,
refugee raft - last human clutch
slipping, all sound swollen.
And we are still startled
by the long winged shadows
crossing the sand long after
the dark gulls have gone.

Abu Salim, Healer

Speaks to spirits
in crowned black letters
strange language a gift of angels in green
he says he remembers only when healing.

Abu Salim touches
those who ache from a spirit
holding to the heart
twisting blood or bone.

For the girl
with a yellow spirit
behind her dry eyes
he burns the dust of red stone

Seven days
in flames, has her breathe
the bitter smoke
to loosen the *jin*

Sways
them both in an orange smoke
until the half-built hut tilts
toward the dry river.

While she sleeps
he bargains with the spirit, says:
Leave through her shoulders
and they will be yours—she will bend.

Leave through her thigh
and she will wander.
But not through her eyes.
They are no good

To you who looked
and back again
on fire. Ash in the air.
She wants water.

Abu Salim says
the spirits can be reasonable
(when she wakes, her back aches,
alone in a goat skin tent beside the hut)

Says the dry river
will flood this winter
(and she is crying)
but there is no telling when.

Sara, Not Sarah

She travels through changing
bodies, each a foreign land,
settles nowhere, follows
no one   this Sara
but a shadow she has not
named   a shadow
                    She starves
until her hips are sharp
her legs too thin
to carry her through.

Later in the moon's cycle
she feeds the hunger
with peelings scavenged
at night and birds that died
en route, then forces it all
to rise.
                    Swollen
her tent flaps wild
would lift with winds
but for the last pegs still holding.

In her mouth
a dry white silence
of tiny stones, silence
of stone.

              Still
when an angel appeared
one day and told her
she would be healed,
Sara laughed, how
she laughed

Where grief hovers

in doorways,
where grief will close its thick wings
around him, bend shoulders to the dark
darkened heart when she is carried out,
he waits the weekend of her dying.

Her wrists, he whispers, *look
at her wrists*, and turns away.
But the last night he strokes
those sharp bones, cuts
through her distance, calls:
Rebecca, open your eyes
and she does.

There, where light enters, turns,
he sees himself as she sees
him—*beloved, o beloved*—
but glimpses, too, all he never knew
of her, now will never know.

Pulling In The Ropes

After both parents died in one year and there were no others who would certainly die before her *Washing down the body* she would remember only this of any story: how he returned to the clan *Scrubbing the skin, cloth over scars* to die. Much later she considered lighting candles *Cloth between toes, over closed eyes* on the date of their death, but the air seemed always too wet, and besides *Brushing the hair soft, clipping the nails* they had died far away *Carrying to the river.* It was not her aloneness, single soup cans, silence in her throat past noon *Pulling in the ropes* which made her lonely. But she worried that her name *Pushing away from shore* not cradled by voices *Washing fingers in the river, watching through the night* would vanish and she couldn't stop remembering *Speaking the stories* how he returned *And singing* to the clan *Not leaving alone* to die.

Notes: from a Sealed Room

and the stars, still and sequestered,
deaf to dark terrene exhalations

I

Hollow beneath the earth's surface

seven stories high
                    its stone sky

weightless in a world of believers:

place of hiding and hidden (heart's
cave, heart's caution—calcareous regions)
half-candle still soft from burning

When last tracks lead to this

nowhere   cacti thick at the cliff

Old World and impassable.

Below:

     antique breathing, terrestial

gods holding(you
      close in a windless

    cradle, stilled sleep
        sleep in the dark

hush

2

Eve of the watchman's night:

fragments fill the house.

what will not be said or imagined.

the mind a boundaried place

in the dark: birds at a border

spreading black wings

rusted grating over a well
wire caging of the cell

and gone in a moment   flying far off

tent city buried in mountain snow
tent city in the graveyard

flying fast off leaving (where I am)

shadows of their wings behind.

3

Across the sea of time and space (sealing

of time and space)

soul ascending to return to stars

But Saturn himself fashioned there

in the deepest ocean   a cave

concealed in it his children   *for eternity*

They have darkened eyes and are muted
                                    motherless

4

(circles *sifr* cypher of absence
in sand

cypress branch in mourning): dear love

no more decoding

White cave that was your heart

walls smoother than skin and
    softer
opened palm revealing fear: perfect
    pearl
in the shadow of a foreign gold ring

crumbles at touch.

I leave (you left) no message in this stone

5

Poor imitative sound: last

syllable lingering
                    ring

lost amid dark marble shine

marble beams
              of a silent moon

in this silent room:

first bomb and there is no knowing.

"Venomous Snake" slithers over airwaves

sirens hurl themselves down corridors.

With fumbling the seal is broken:

Gas mask   Black rubber straps

Black ash   History
                    unbelieved.

6

Fear a silent creature at the threshold where

gas may seep through.

We tape door-rim and keyhole crush

wet towels into white spaces cover

windows with thick plastic crouch

by inner walls caves in corners.

Obedient in fabrications of safety

atropin needle talc radiowaves

silent.

But only the walls will fall, this warfare

conventional   coeval with creation:

the baby to be born is still.

7

Soft imagining

too narrow for rough sorrow: *little girl*

> *little girl in all your dark greed*
> *pretend, pretend and pretend.*

Voice dressed in white at midday dressed

in borrowed white at midnight

never whiter

> *stones under moonlight in an emptied land*
> *bones that will stay buried   stars that are falling*
> *unseen*

at first siren :

8

Bellowing across open spaces

(imprint on a blinded eye:

burnt tanks half bodies

unburied in a dead

gulley imprint in

sand white blaze

of sun)

There. That voice: gray bird of dust

circling itself and nothing

across a bare plain

to nowhere

as foretold

9

In the silence of after

I was undone:

ululating siren marked a place

of possibility become

real

(each threshold sacred
every passing through door and gate
a tenuous prayer).

In the silence of after

I am undone   weeks and months

with my voice lost to a doorway

cave entrances   imagined spaces

dark
        nest in a
                    salt sea

10

Deep in a land that devours its inhabitants:

stone solitude, stone silence.

Seek safety where you can, scarab

beetle, softest baby   your breathing

only sound in this wide chamber   (Mother

my mother

has disappeared, flown(red bird

red bird, what do you see?)

to her own dying mother's side

And she, my mother, is howling still

across open spaces

sealed time later: her mother waited

not for her

but for the fondest boy to return

to die.   Her breasts heavy

with milk (my milk   little lamb, scarab beetle, softest
   baby)
                         outside that hospital room,
      not yet knowing

she would not be the one to close the eyes of her dead

not be triply blessed   triply beloved

II

In a sealed room

last word slipped(stripped)

away.

Next bomb fell in the sea

another lost to the desert:

jeeps sped off in search of

Love, the craving

that was hunger has passed.

They'll not see the cave

nor the gray bird at the entrance

perched on the mastic tree

pecking itself into silence.

                you ask
why here, in the high north,
perched on peaks and slopes,
open to the sky's full weight
of fringed clouds
and bombs, why here?
We stopped on our way to the sea
and stayed: I remember
nothing more, but the stars
told stories, pointed
nowhere. We built homes
on stilts, terraced the hillside,
and the mountain now wears rings
of red dirt paths round her,
wedded as we are.
We bathe in these mists,
our salt is of stone, and we carry
this sky on our shoulders, heavy
and warm. In winter, wrapped in shrouds
of white silence and space, there is
no escape: god follows, bears down
with the weight of a child
in your arms, on your mind.
Our youngest carried dreams
of a side unseen, climbed over
a barbed wire fence last spring
and stepped on a mine.
The soil is not fertile, too many rocks,
and too many years are meagre.

Muscles ache, and the heart—
but we are mountain people,
we cannot live on flat land.

Comments on *AZIMUTH*

Meditative as they are, with syntax lapping at itself, the phrases terse but musical, the lines borrowing and extending a talismanic lexicon, with a quieter, parenthetical voice modifying the quiet, insistent voice, with meanings catching in the inflection of the silence, Rachel Tzvia Back's poems are psalms on a journey. While Milton's Satan finds in the lowest deep a lower deep, Back finds in shrouds of white silence and space that god follows. Rereading *Azimuth*, I felt (again!) the hair on the back of my neck rising.

–Forrest Gande

With grace and gravity, with a gentle, quiet tenacity, Rachel Tzvia Bac brings the poetics of indeterminacy to bear on Israel's over-determine landscape. Her verse hurts as the land itself has been hurt: its rippling musi is delicate and achieved, its evocation of intimacy stunning. As political as is personal, *Azimuth* shows us, again, how history and linguistic horizor meet, and who we are or might be before them.

–Peter Co

Rachel Tzvia Back, born in 1960, has lived in Israel since 1981. Her poetry and translations have appeared in numerous journals. Back resides in the Western Galilee.

ISBN 1878818

THE SHEEP MEADOW PRESS
RIVERDALE-ON-HUDSON, NEW YORK

9 781878 818